MW01181092

THE SEVEN PRINCIPLES OF SUCCESS

by Clarence Mason "Weaver"

Published by Mason Media Company
Copyright © 2018 by Clarence Mason "Weaver"
ISBN: 978-0-9744423-6-5

CLARENCE A. MASON "WEAVER"
SEVEN PRINCIPLES OF SUCCESS

Success is a verb, not a noun.
It is based upon what you are doing,
not what you are thinking.

No one's opinion of you should mean more
to you than your opinion of you.

Wisdom comes not from the journey,
but from the experiences along the way.

If you compromise on your principles,
you have none.

If you are not willing to sacrifice,
you are not willing to succeed.

A dream is something you think you can do;
a goal is something you are doing.

Truth is eternal and unchangeable and does
not submit itself to the thoughts, hopes,
or actions of man.

1971

Being discharged from the U. S. Navy. Poor, disabled, unemployable High School Dropout.

1975

Addressing my U.C. Berkeley Political Science Graduation Class.

INTRODUCTION

On August 11, 1971 at 9:05 a.m., I became a permanently disabled American. I was a poor, Black, unemployable high school dropout. By August 1975, I had earned multiple college degrees and had started a journey to financial independence, because I knew that working 30 years was impossible. By August 1981, I had NO JOB, JUST INCOME.

Yes, going to Berkeley was rough. I was in constant pain and consistently on pain medications. Studying was rough for the same reasons. We all have choices and mine were easy to see. Either suffer quickly through the pain or have a life of poverty and helplessness. When the burden got too hard and I was contemplating another course, I would take a drive to a local liquor store, where I could see many individuals who had already given up on life. So, I would decide: let's get to work!

What is success? The definition depends upon your goals and your efforts. Success is not really associated with things or achievements. Those are the expressions of your achievements, but not the expressions of your success. Success is comfort, independence, control, influence, and confidence.

The baby who learns by failing is first motivated to try. Progress is natural, and therefore motivation is natural, too. Motivation is the result of the right perspective and the right environment. With knowledge, you can change your perspective. With tools, you can change your environment. This book will help you to acquire the knowledge and tools to both change your life and to lead others to success.

The truth is that the only real motivation is SELF motivation. Although I am called a "motivational speaker," I really inspire people to dream and hope. I can't make you get up and start a business or read a book; it has to be in you to do that already. All I can do is reinforce the knowledge and desire that already exists within you by using inspirational stories and examples from my life and the lives of others.

If you tell people what they already know, it builds their confidence that their beliefs are correct. Believing that you are right about something will serve to drive you to prove that you are right. Working to prove that you are right will force you to reject things that are contrary and embrace things

2

that support your work. The force that drives you to prove that which is right within you is called "motivation."

No one can implant that type of drive within you, so no one other than you can truly motivate you. However, although motivation comes from within, the elements you need to foster and support motivation are external. Just like the baby who wants to walk, you must know that it is possible (seeing others walk) and you must be in the right environment (open space). Once the knowledge and environment are both intact, a healthy, normal baby will make attempts at walking; he or she will then be motivated to try.

This also means that the forces which hinder motivation are also external. Ignorance is the opposite of knowledge. A negative environment is the opposite of a positive environment. In order to motivate yourself, you simply have to change those external factors and allow motivation to germinate naturally.

Success is like a lonely rock on the beach. If you do not associate with other rocks you are subject to the constant waves. You may be determined to become a mountain one day. You can stand in defiance against the waves but they will come. They will work not on your strength, but on your foundation. They will wear away at the foundation of your marriage, children, job, finances, health and fear. They will eventually wear away the sands around your feet and your dreams will collapse into a nightmare of despair.

However, if you associate with other solid rocks, you will stand on the beach like a SEA WALL, deflecting the constant waves.

The waves will come at their own time. You'll have high tides and low tides. You'll have waves affected by the storms in your life. Some waves will be sent as storm surges, others will come as an afternoon swell. But they will come, and your response to them will be determined by your preparation.

If you have weak associations, the waves of life will be deflected off of your life unto the lives of the sand and the people around you. Their foundations will collapse and yours will be weakened because of your association with them. The stronger your associations, the stronger your foundation.

I tried many jobs because most people would not hire someone with a physical disability. I could not tolerate prolonged walking, sitting or standing. What does that leave— lying in bed? I could do all of those things if I could change positions during the day. If I could stand up, sat down or take a short walk, I could work all day.

What I could not do was sit all day, walk all day or stand all day. That placed a pretty good limit on which jobs I could do. I had jobs as a contract negotiator, private business consultant, driving instructor, and many more. I tried my own businesses in video production, jewelry, cosmetics, radio talk show host, and newspaper columnist.

The hardest job I had was as a door-to-door vending machine salesman. The sale of vending machines required getting to the decision maker of the company and convincing him to spend $4,000 on a cigarette machine. It required getting past the people hired to keep people away from the owner. This job had a great deal of rejection. Most of the sales were preceded by a barrage of rejections.

Eventually, though, I became one of the top sales persons in the area, by using a special technique that has worked in many areas of my life. It was based upon how I approached the inevitable rejection. Every morning I knew where I was going to work, which business I was going to approach and that I would be rejected all day long. But I had also determined that for every 300 rejections from qualified people, there was one sale.

You could make a pretty good living on one vending machine sale a week, so all I had to do was collect 300 rejections a week to make my goal. I started looking at rejections as a good thing. Like a miner panning for gold, each qualified rejection got me closer to the mother lode. I became pleased with the rejection and looked forward to the next one.

I made sales from my rejections. When I got in front of a qualified owner and he rejected my idea, I would always ask about other business people he knew that may benefit from a vending machine. Now if he found me annoying, he would give me the number of his competitor to go and irritate him. If he found me informative and easy to say no to, he would refer me to his business friends that might have use for a machine.

It became clear that gaining success was

connected to gaining rejections. I had a technique to measure the rejections I sought every day. When I left home in the morning I would carry 100 small seeds in my pocket. I would have 50 in the right pocket and 50 in the left. My route would be planned the prior evening and I would always work my plan.

Every time I got a rejection I would walk out of the business and take one seed out of my left pocket and flip it up into the air. I would seek rejection after rejection and do the same thing. I would not allow myself to stop for lunch until I had emptied my left pocket with the rejected seeds. It was the same with the right pocket and I would not go home that evening until I had completed my job, getting 100 rejections in a day.

It was a very successful technique that I have shared with groups all over the nation. Not only are you planting seeds for your own success, each seed is an anti-rejection medication for your psyche. With this technique I seldom got only one sale. When I finally made a sale I would speak to the friends, competitors and associates of the "winner" and proceed to sale his church, social group and even building landlord.

People like success and successful people like to be around other successful people. I planted a lot of seeds around this country and they have brought me a lot of success.

This book will serve to reinforce what you already know to be true, teach you some things that you didn't know, and describe the proper, healthy environment for motivation and progress.

THE FIVE REASONS WE DESIRE FREEDOM

COMFORT. Don't be comfortable where you are, but be comforted in your ability to affect where you are. Comfort, while in the stress, pain and disappointments, is not comfort from the stress, pain and disappointments. You should have the ability to relax and face whatever life brings. Be able to enjoy the good times and get through the bad, without stress, anxiety or emotional capital. Every problem you face and survive is a brick in the foundation of your life. The more overcoming, the more bricks in that foundation. Ask a long-time married couple about the keys to a successful marriage and they will recite the problems they overcame. They will not talk about the vacations, grandkids or business success, but the problems they faced together, conquered together, resisted together, and the confidence they built in each other and with each other. Comfort is your peace of mind, knowing you are prepared to handle most of life's situations. Buying a home with the ability to finance it yourself, will make your conversation with the banker much more comfortable.

INDEPENDENCE. Not needing nor seeking the approval of others with decisions in your life. You will always need consultations from advisors and mentors, but the decisions should be yours. You are the ONLY person guaranteed to spend every second of your life with every decisions you make. It is important to have wise council and advisers around you, but your decisions should be made independent of the wishes of others. Being in the position of disappointing the boss, losing that relationship, and still honoring your principles, brings peace of mine. Making that decision when it conflicts with the principles of others, is independence.

On the morning of September 11, 2001, a friend of mine was with his wife at a Manhattan hotel near the World Trade Center. His financial institution had spent $750,000 setting up a meeting with him in Tower One of The World Trade Center. They were hoping to use his wealth for a business deal which was promising to be very lucrative for him also. He woke up that morning and "just did not feel like going." He rolled over, stayed in bed, turned on the TV and watched the tower collapse. Most of us would have been too concerned about our reputation, disappointing the bank or losing out financially. His independence and freedom saved his life that morning. Be so free that you can walk away from any deal, even a good one.

CONTROL. The expression of power. Success requires you to accumulate control over your life, securing the power to direct, redirect and make sudden, controlled changes in direction. When September 11, 2001 happened, many people were stranded across the country when Airlines were grounded. Rental cars, buses, trains and hotels were all full, unavailable, or closed. Many people could not get home and families were separated because of a national crisis. I knew a gentleman, stranded 800 miles from his pregnant wife. While millions of stranded travelers worried about who was going to get them home, he walked into a used car lot, pulled out his credit card and purchased a car.

INFLUENCE. People are influenced by you because of the power you can bring to a situation. A successful reputation will prompt others to seek your advice. It doesn't mean power or strength; it means others value your wisdom and experience. Wise people would rather learn from your mistakes than their own. Make sure you go through life paying attention to the successes and failures of life. That gives you wisdom and wisdom is sought by others.

CONFIDENCE. Confidence comes from the experiences of making mistakes, learning solutions, and having the ability to repeat successes. If someone gave me an old car to drive across country, I would not have the confidence to make the journey. But if I was an experienced mechanic and was towing a trailer with equipment, parts and tools, I would have great confidence in driving that car across country. It is the effort that gives confidence. Failing or succeeding gives you more confidence than the person who has never tried. The more you try the more confidence you are going to have.

THE SEVEN PRINCIPLES OF SUCCESS

PRINCIPLE ONE:
SUCCESS IS A VERB

Success is a verb, not a noun.
It is based upon what you are doing
and not what you are thinking.

Laying in the hospital on August 11, 1971, I found my career path completely disrupted. I was a trained Navy welder, pipe-fitter and ship-fitter. A dirty, hard skill-set, very lucrative in civilian life. But 2,800 pounds of steel, iron and aluminum plates falling on you will make hard, manual work impossible.

As I lay in the hospital bed, all of the doctors and staff were telling me what I could not do. I heard them as background noise as I was concentrating on what I COULD do.

I did not have the stamina, strong back, skills or even motivation that I once possessed. But what I did have was a brain and confidence in its ability to figure out this new situation in my life.

I had no choice and no other options. I could sink or swim, become dependent or independent, take care of myself or allow others to take care of me. What type of lifestyle did I want and what type did I see coming? Was I going to reset my goals to reflect my condition or recondition my situation to meet my set goals?

So, I laid in that hospital bed, ignoring the conditions and restrictions on my life played out by the experts, and began planning the next 60 years of living with myself, based on the decisions I'd begun making about myself.

I wasn't "disabled;" I was just "unable" to serve the Navy anymore. However, I still had full control of serving myself. I discovered that SUCCESS was a verb. It was not dependent on what I thought of myself, but on what I was doing for myself. I needed clarity, support and measurable goals.

1. **Change the language.**

   You are what you call yourself. I never called myself "disabled" I never answered to it and did not hang out with those who did. I called myself a "student" before I entered college and a "businessman" before I entered business.

2. **Pain teaches you and failure teaches you.**

   There are no wrong decisions because they all teach you lessons. What's wrong is not trying, allowing others to discourage you, and failing to recognize that success is a verb and not a noun. What's important is not what you are but what you are doing.

3. **Change who you surround yourself with.**

   Family and old friends may not be going where you are going. There's nothing wrong with them; they are just on a different path. Spend your time with people who you can learn from and who you can teach. If they are not heading in the same direction as you, they should not be around you. Just because you hung out in high school does not mean you will hang out in the Board Room. Yes, they will talk about you.

4. Knowledge vs. Ignorance

A. Knowledge: understanding, clarity, wisdom. Courage is the experience of victory; you never lose, it's just the cost of learning. Confidence is what results when you learn that victory is won by overcoming. Leadership is what results when others see the courage and confidence and they follow, if you are going somewhere.

B. Ignorance: unaware, no vision, no confidence. Fear freezes you, does not motivate you. When you walk to the kitchen in the middle of the night and you hear a noise, you freeze. Self-doubt means accepting your position or condition with no ambition. Fellowship is seeking the comfort of those showing confidence, accept being around like-minded people, sharing the same principles.

PRINCIPLE TWO:
YOUR OPINION OF YOU

No one's opinion of you should mean more to you than your opinion of you.

Many people chimed in on why I could not make a living, attend Berkeley, and certainly why I could not start my own business. They all meant well and all had their reasons for buying into my failure. I had run into these same people all of my life and it always seemed to be connected with jealousy, competition, and an attitude of "If Mason could do it, then I must be lazy."

Others will tell you that you're too fat, addicted, damaged or inherently poor, to make things work for yourself. If you believe them, they are correct. But no one told you that you could crawl, walk, or ride a bike. But you were determined to do it and your determination overcame all of it. No one in my family had owned a business, how could I do it?

It does not matter what others have done; someone has to be the first. You can do whatever you get excited about doing. You are what you call yourself, not what others call you.

I once had a meeting with a very successful manufacturer of Black beauty products. I asked him what gave him the courage to launch such a venture in a small White Southern town in the 1960s, with no background and no support? Didn't anyone tell you that a Black man cannot be the largest employer in this White town, own the biggest hotel, build and name the Civic Center after his mother and donate the land for the Junior College, and still build an internationally renowned company? His response was classic: "I guess I did not get the memo."

I then asked him how the business owners and financial institutions treat him? He was undereducated, had a learning disability, and a speech impediment. "When I go to the bank, they don't know if I "is rich," "be rich," or "are rich," but my money, influence, employment, philanthropy, and investments will benefit even those working against me."

You are not what people call you; you are what you call yourself. I am a successful motivational speaker, even though I am a stutterer. I debated issues on radio and television, even though I speak too fast for most people. I am an author of many books, but do not like writing. What you are is irrelevant, what you do will make you into a free person.

YOU CANNOT WIN IF YOU DO NOT BEGIN!

How often do we stop ourselves from beginning? We talk ourselves out of it because of pre-determined ideas and magical thinking. Some people think their skin color is a barrier to success in America and they will give you a number of valid reasons for believing it. They will cite past discrimination, legal barriers and social struggles to indicate that the pigmentation of their skin is a strong barrier to overcome. This fear could keep them from the competitive structure which prepares them to succeed. One may not go to school because of the fear of skin color barriers. Why try to get a job; the skin color barrier will stop me. But skin color, like all other external and internal obstacles, only limits you if you let it.

Let's take that person who is convinced that the color of their skin has become an overwhelming barrier for them. Let's pretend that their skin color disappears, and they now have the same pigmentation as the majority of Americans. Are we saying that all other Americans would now support them in their efforts to compete in America?

In other words, when they go for that job interview with people with equal skin pigmentation, will they find them supportive? Will the other job seekers encourage them in their application? Will they give them a chance for the same job? Of course not!

If you entered a business looking for a sales position and saw only women working there, and you were a man, would you give up? Would you say, "They would never give a sales position to a man; they only want women here?" If you were crippled do you think those walking would not buy a car from you? There will always be differences among us. Every job sought, every sale presented is a competition against someone else. There will always be someone wanting that job or that sale. They would rather you talk yourself out of it so they can win. It does not matter if you use your skin color, gender, age or accent, if you can talk yourself out of the sale, they win.

When I graduated from Berkeley I applied for a job with the Department of Energy. There were three jobs open and over 2,500 applications. It took eight months of interviewing before the decision was made to hire me and the others. I was there to compete and win not just to show up. I fully expected to be one of the finalists and did not allow any negative thinking to enter my mind. This was my job and the other applicants were simply in my way.

I learned that working towards a goal may be more important than reaching that goal. When I laid in that hospital bed in 1971, I was a high school dropout with a goal of being an attorney. That meant getting my high school diploma, starting college and passing the Law School Admission Test (LSAT).

If my goal was to finish high school or enter college I would have stopped at that point. But because I was looking to law school, I kept on going. It was not until I had received my high school diploma, finished Berkeley and passed the LSAT did I change my goals. But that goal from 1971 turned a high school dropout into a UC Berkeley graduate.

Success will not be found in your comfort zone.

Set your goals way past your comfort zone. Set your goals high enough for a better view of your options. Have fun and be persistent; the journey is great. See you at the top!

Learn to LISTEN. Others have information you need. No matter how insignificant they are to your business, they have something to offer. Listen and Silent have the same letters. You cannot do one correctly, without doing the other, correctly.

1. Develop a clear, distinctive self-identity. Know who you are, where you are going and how to recognize when you get there.

2. Expect the obstacles; they are the fertilizers to grow your success.

3. If you fall off schedule, don't fall off course.

4. Recognize every small success and every small failure. Pay attention.

5. Keep good notes; folks are going to enjoy reading your book about success.

PRINCIPLE THREE:
WISDOM

*Wisdom comes, not from the journey,
but from the experiences along the way.*

You don't have to tell me a disabled high school dropout could graduate from UC Berkeley with multiple degrees in less than three years because I have already experienced that. But NO ONE believed it was possible, including the college guidance counselor. So now I can tell young folks how I did it and help many people get through college early and start the journey of making a living. I have the wisdom of my experiences.

A few years after my marriage, my wife decided she too wanted to go to college. She had the benefit of my experience and finished early. I was able to guide her through the classes because I understood. We stopped calling her a Technician for AT&T and started calling her a STUDENT. I became a student too, because the household had to become a dorm for studying; no social life and no non-student friends. We placed the graduation date on the calendar and told folks years ahead of time to plan vacations to come witness and help us celebrate.

You are what you call yourself. I failed 11 times in business. But number 12, 13 and 14 proved to be well worth the efforts. I could not stand, walk, travel or even sit for very long. I had to find a way to stay engaged and create income within these limitations. I knew it was there and I knew it was achievable. I had to fail in order to succeed. If you knew failing 100 times would bring you enough wisdom and experience to provide a great business success, would you keep trying?

I knew a young man in California who started a Foreclosure business, buying homes at court auctions. He did his homework and researched each auction. His team became very good at identifying the best deals and he started sharing his knowledge with other competitors at the auction. Soon his reputation was so well established and his information was so valuable, that others would not bid against him and this allowed him to get homes at a very good price. He shared his knowledge and that made money for his competitors and they valued it enough to allow him to have what he wanted. He built the largest Foreclosure company in the area because he shared his knowledge.

The winner of a race is the one who crosses the finish line first, not the one who looks the best, starts the fastest, is in the best shape, is better educated, or is more motivated. It is the one who figures out where the finish line is and the best way to get there. Stay Focused.

I remember my first multimillion-dollar government contract negotiation. As the lead government negotiator, I was very excited about having my first large contract. The opposing negotiator had experiences as a contract specialist for longer than I had been living. The contract was a five-year renewal of a long term nuclear research and development project.

As we entered the fee negotiation stage, I was reminded of the fact that this negotiator had always won an increase in profit from the government. I did not think they needed it this time. After evaluating his proposal, I called for the fee/profit negotiation meeting.

My first question to him was: "I have read your proposal. That cannot be the best you can do. You do not really expect me to accept this, do you?" Dead silence fell over the room. I looked at him politely; he stared back intensely as we both waited. No one moved; there wasn't even a change in posture. We continued to stare for at least two very long minutes.

There were eight others in the room, including both attorneys, engineers, project managers and an assistant contract specialist, and all were silent. Finally, the opposing negotiator sighed and smiled. With a nod of acknowledgment, he said: "Well we were late with our final report last year and did not meet all of our goals, so we'll take off 1% from our fee.

I sat quietly and turned the pages on my contract book. After a few pages were turned, I looked up at him again, in silence. He stared at me and the page I was on, looked down at the exact same page in his book, and sighed again. "Well, sir, I guess that cost overrun last year really hurt us. If we reduce our fee by 5% would that get us to the table?"

It was checkmate. For the first time in 15 years, this major government contractor had failed to receive an increase in fee, and had, instead, agreed to a reduction in fee. My silence forced him to negotiate against himself. You will always win when they negotiate against themselves. Silence is always your friend. Do not be afraid of it. Use it often.

1. Learn as much from the mistakes as from the successes.

2. Develop a good group of business friends, competitors and wise council. Every great athlete had an adversary. Muhammad Ali had Joe Frasier. Larry Bird had Magic Johnson. You need competition to learn how to earn.

3. Success brings responsibility. You must have an avenue to teach, motivate, inspire and promote others. The teacher learns more than the student. The more you help others, the stronger you become. The more successful your profession is, the bigger the revenue pie is. The bigger the revenue pie, the more your share of that pie will be. Grow your industry as well as your business.

4. Never stop learning. Write, read, debate, discuss and teach. It gives you confidence, wisdom and recognition. You must know the product, and

that of your competitors. You must know them thoroughly and deeply.

When I sold cars, it was very important that I not only knew my vehicles but that of my competition. Often, customers knew more about the cars that they're interested in, and the competitor's cars, than the salesperson. As a salesperson, you must have an in-depth knowledge of your cars as well as the other car your customer liked.

One day, a gentleman came into the dealership with his wife, looking for a Nissan Maxima. She wanted the Toyota Camry and was already sold on it.

The cars were similar, but they also had some major differences. My Maxima was clearly superior in some areas and the Toyota, in others. While test driving the Maxima, I gave my usual speech about being their consultant not their salesman. I wanted them to know that I was interested in them getting the car they wanted, not just the car I wanted them to have. They were very skeptical of this because I worked for Nissan, not Toyota.

To prove my sincerity, I offered to let them test drive my car to the Toyota dealership and I would help them make the decision to buy the Camry over my car. We drove to the nearby Toyota dealership and I walked in with them. The salesman was not as knowledgeable about the Camry or my Maxima as I was, and he did not know I worked as a Nissan salesman.

I asked him questions about the Camry and had him point out its flaws. I also asked him questions about options on the Camry that I knew were inferior to the Maxima. By the time we had finished, both customers were sold on the Maxima. The sale was the result of one thing: not being afraid of failure. The customer was leaning towards the competition so I went with them into the heart of the competition and won the sale on the competitor's territory.

You must understand the reasons for rejections:

a. They just do not want nor need it. No matter how good you are, you cannot sell ice to an Eskimo.

b. They do not want to think you are taking advantage of them.

c. They do not believe in the product nor see themselves successful in utilizing it.

d. You are selling it as a benefit to you, not to them.

PRINCIPLE FOUR:
PRINCIPLES

*If you compromise on your principles,
you have none.*

Ask yourself these two questions: What issue would you stand on, even if you knew it would cost you your business? What level of success would you pay for with the love and respect of your family? Those answers will identify your principles. You must have a published set of principle beliefs that everyone doing business with you understands and recognizes. They will watch you and check you, but they will also respect you. Everyone should have a personal "Resolution" to guide their personal and business existence. Here is mine:

"I Pledge to: Shed light on the truth. Confront the lie. Inform those seeking truth. Organize those opposing the lie. Judge results, not intentions. Pray for all of you! Stay with a few of you!"
— Proverb 29-2

"When the righteous are in authority, the people rejoice: but when the wicked beareth rule, the people mourn."

You cannot have balance and tolerance.

Only logic and truth should prevail not, balance and tolerance. There are some things we should want as much as possible without balance. Most of us want as much money as possible without trying to "balance" it out with poverty. We desire as much good health as possible without worrying about balancing it out with sickness. In our personal lives, we want warmth in the winter and coolness in the summer.

We do not seek a balance because it would require accepting negatives when we do not have to. I have had to leave business agreements when asked to do something against my principles.

Your family and friends know your principles and they see you bending them for profit and it ruins the very reason you are in business. Your principles will make some uncomfortable and they will distance themselves from you. Others will see those principles and stay closer to you. Your support group will be like-minded, focused, and self-strengthening. The more principled your team, the stronger your team.

Once, I tried to give a guy my condo. This was a no money down, no qualifying deal for him. We had purchased the condo a few months earlier for no money down, and the tax savings was all we really wanted from it. Selling the condo, paying the brokerage fees and capital gains, and keeping it on the market after 30 days just was not worth the few dollars we would gain.

So, my wife and I placed an ad in the local paper and looked for someone to give the condo to. This gentleman answered the ad and we were really impressed by him at first. He was trying to better himself and was a hard worker. We made the deal with him to take over our payments and put his name on our loan.

The deal was set and he even started painting the condo while we exchanged paperwork. One evening, he gave me a call, and he was very upset. Someone (probably a friend who did not own any property) had told him it was a bad deal. This friend had "checked" the records and found I was "selling" the condo for more than I had paid for it. Imagine that, I was actually being accused of making a profit on the sale of my property.

It was not even true. This friend had looked up the county assessor's appraised value of the condo, which never reflects the actual value, nor the cost. The guy came over to my home, still upset. I even showed him the loan paperwork, confirming that his friend was mistaken. But it was too late; his pride and embarrassment would only allow him to continue arguing with me.

But why would I argue in favor of giving my condo to someone? I let him out of the deal and he left. I made one phone call to another investor and the condo was sold before this guy got back home. Too bad he allowed others to talk him out of the greatest deal he would ever have.

When I applied for a job opening with the U.S. Department of Energy, competition was very high. This intern program had produced most of the senior managers at the department and thousands of applicants applied. Most of us were qualified and only a few had an obvious edge. At this level of competition your college, grades, past job experience, and IQ were just as impressive as those of hundreds of others in the group. You needed an edge and everyone tried to find it.

After months of tests and pre-interviews, the original 2,500 applicants were reduced to 35, and we were called in for interviews. We were all from great schools: Stanford, Harvard, Berkeley — where I was from — and all were qualified. At this level, they could have drawn straws and had a good candidate.

When I was called in to be interviewed by the Director of Personnel, I arrived and sat in her office. I always look around an office for signs of the person's personality. I quickly noticed baby pictures, books on baby care and even a deflated balloon from a baby gift, on a plant. It was obvious that the Director of Personnel had just had a baby, or that someone in the family had. It was obvious that this baby was an important part of her life.

When the Director of Personnel came into the room, I also noticed that she was on the older side of child bearing years. It became clear that this middle-aged woman had just given birth to her first child and was still very excited about it. Well it just so happened that my first son was only six months old at the time and I was equally excited. Guess what we spent most of the time talking about?

I had connected with her on a very personal level and she naturally thought I was just a little more sensitive, intelligent, and easier to get along with than most of the other serious, academic robots she had interviewed with.

Do not forget: most people are just as qualified for the job as you are. Personnel hire people who fit into the office mix and who will add their unique personality to the success of the company.

Every time I called the Department to check or provide more information, I would ask the Director about her child (by name) and tell her about mine. Of course I got the position and will never know how much this helped to close the deal, but how could it have hurt? Knowing as much as you can about the emotional buttons of those you are doing business with can only help you.

PRINCIPLE FIVE:
SACRIFICE

*If you are not willing to sacrifice,
you are not willing to succeed.*

*Every plan must include
a list of sacrifices.*

If you do not know what you will sacrifice, you do not know what you want. Don't start because of what your grandmother did, start because of what your grandchildren will do. It is too hard; you miss too much and give too much to work, just for your own satisfaction. It will not be worth the long hours, lonely decisions, and constant pressure just to enjoy the success for yourself. Most of us need a reason to conquer the world. Find yours, and allow it to motivate you during the rough times.

You must be willing to make the sacrifice to gain what you are looking for. It will cost you. You may have to give up television, hanging out with your friends, going on vacations, or going out to dinner. You must clearly understand the sacrifices required and you and your spouse should be willing to expend some cost for the goals.

You have heard the term "delayed gratification," but it is very hard to handle with children and responsibility. You can't delay medical help to your children, but you can delay that NEW car, vacation or expensive purchase.

My wife and I started planning for our retirement early. Retirement is the most expensive item of your future. You know it is a time of limited income but higher healthcare. It is also the time when you have the greatest accumulation of debt. You now have the most expensive home you have ever owned, and you've just finished paying for your children's education and weddings. So just as you get the home, college tuition, weddings and traveling, you reduce your income, quit your job, and call it Retirement.

About 15 years before we retired, my wife asked me to stop buying her jewelry. She had more than she could use, and it was more desirable to put the money towards other things. She also asked me to buy her fewer expensive coats, perfumes, and hats. (Still working on the shoes).

We have traveled to 47 states, all over the Caribbean and Mexico, and have decided that we have traveled enough. We saw the quick depreciation of our cars and other toys and decided to buy old, instead of new. So, for 15 years we've had extra money to invest, yet still enjoy a very active lifestyle and a very peaceful, relaxed retirement, because we delayed so much. Those cars and toys would have all been gone by now, but the quality of life for a retired couple is unimaginable to you younger folks.

Did you know that 85% of your entire medical expense occurs during the last six months of your life? We now have grandchildren, children and ourselves to take care of. We've had to prepare for the most expensive time of our life — without jobs.

As you earn income in your business, don't forget to PAY YOUR SELF first. Save, enroll in 401k programs, invest, and do it routinely. Invest in good times and bad, invest wisely and consistently. Prepare for those expensive retirement years, because they are coming. Not only are they coming, they will surprise you. Even though you can plan for them, you must be ready to change course and deploy your wisdom, because those retirement years will be full of things you didn't plan for.

Stand on the shoulders of those who have come before you, but not for those who have come before you. Do it for your grandchildren and their children. That is the only way it will be worth it.

The key to success is SERVICE!

If you are not willing to sacrifice, you are not willing to succeed. Sacrifice for your family, community and humanity, never for yourself. You would be better off buying Nike stock than Nike shoes. One will last a few months the other for generations.

My granddaughters and I were looking over some old photo albums of mine. One noticed all of the nice new cars I drove 20, 30 years ago. She asked why I had a Cadillac, Jaguar, Mercedes, BMW, a boat, motorhome, and a few custom vans. But now my cars are very old. "What happened?" I answered: "GRANDCHILDREN." I am no longer worrying about the type of cars I am driving, but the type of cars my grandchildren will drive. It's called Legacy!

I once visited a very successful businessman

and stayed in his guest home. This man had been in business for many years and had achieved overwhelming success. His guest home had a private lake, tennis court, swimming pool and spa for his visitors. The home had a ten-car garage, with luxury cars and trucks available for the visitors, and the property included a private three-hole golf course for those so inclined.

But what impressed me most was the owner. After making sure I was comfortable on his grand estate, he excused himself. He had to drive two hours away, to show his business plan to strangers, just to give them a dream of success. This very successful business man, with many people available to travel for him, was still being motivated by a servant's heart. His success was not based upon how persuasive he was nor his charismatic power. His success, and that of all of his leaders, was based upon serving the public. They believed their business was a benefit to all who saw the plan. They did not let their poverty nor their wealth throw them off course. It was never about the money; it was always about changing people and the country.

If poverty had motivated that businessman, he

would have failed after financial success, because he would have stopped trying. If financial success was his motivation, he would have sent others out for that late evening meeting. He went himself and left all of his luxury, because there was one more person needing help. I do not know any real successful people in any field who do not have the heart of a servant.

If You Are Not Willing to Sacrifice, You Are Not Willing to Succeed.

What are you willing to lose to achieve your goals? I once consulted with someone on his financial matters. He was praying for help in overcoming a particular financial challenge. It was measurable and we knew how much money would be needed to overcome this emotionally draining financial problem. Once we analyzed the client's finances, I came to a very interesting conclusion. The amount of money needed to solve the problem was available to him through his own resources. He had the cash on hand to solve the problem. But there was another problem: he had ear-marked the money for something else.

He had plans for that money and did not want

to sacrifice, to take care of his immediate problem. He lacked confidence in making the money back. He considered his success in obtaining his money just luck, not the result of hard work. His success was repeatable if he overcome his doubts. He had already reached his goals, but they interfered with the plans he already made for the cash on hand.

What he lacked was not cash, he lacked confidence in replacing the cash he had on hand. What else could we conclude? If he had confidence in his ability to restore his savings, he would have had no problem in spending it to solve his immediate financial needs. This guy reminded me of the person lost in the desert who died of thirst with water still in the canteen. Use what you have for the current need; you will gain future resources for future needs. We are not willing to sacrifice what we have so we do not gain what we need.

Every plan must include a list of sacrifices. If you do not know what you will sacrifice, you do not know what you want. When you were an infant you could play with all of the other boys and girls in the sandlot. Your only problems were who would share their toys with you. But every child had most things in common. A few years later you get a bike and your best friend from the sandlot gets skates. You and your best friend could still play together with the bike and skates but there were some differences. You may have found more friends with bikes and played with them also, but you still kept your friend with the skates. As you get a little older you get a car and your best friend from the sandlot gets a motorcycle. You can still meet your friend at dances and ball games, but your friendship starts to pull apart because he has more motorcycle friends and you have car friends.

Now you're in high school and you want to go to medical school and your best friend from the sandlot wants to be a Rock star. While you need to go to the library at night he wants to go to the clubs to meet band managers and agents. You seldom see each other and eventually lose contact.

What happened? Why did you and your friend pull apart? Because as your interests changed you had to change your friends and associates. You had to surround yourself with people with similar goals. You had to acquaint yourself with those who would encourage you and work with you.

Your Rock star friend would not understand why you cannot come with him to auditions when you needed to study and keep your grades up, but your other pre-med students would. So, you change your friends and sacrifice your social life for your goals and plans.

If you plan on being successful, you must associate with other people who have the same drive and goals. It does not matter if it's a marriage, career or religion, you must associate with winners if you plan on being one.

As soon as you make that decision, your sandlot friends will not understand. They will accuse you of changing and even selling out from some mythical code of sandlot friends. If you succumb to this pressure you will lose. If you let others dictate your goals, ambitions, standards or level of success you will lose. Success takes sacrifice and change. If you will not sacrifice and are unwilling to change, you will always be the baby in the sandlot needing someone to change him.

I once witnessed a fight in a restaurant between two men. One was very large and powerful and the other was of average stature. The big guy had a reputation for bullying people and he was very intimidating. The little guy had stood up to this bully on some manner and they were standing toe to toe.

The big bully swung with all of his strength and knocked the little guy to the floor. He stood over him for a second, huffing and puffing, looking as mean and proud of himself as ever. Then his look turned to concern and even a little fear. This little guy that had just taken this guy's best punch, but was climbing back to his feet. He was down but not out; he was off his feet but not off his goal. The stronger guy backed off and gave ground. The bully had given all he had — strength and power. The little guy won on determination. You see, the bully did not want to deal with this man's determination. The bigger guy could win on strength and intimidation but this other guy wanted to make him win on heart.

In sales, business and family life, heart is the strongest element. It can either lead you, or keep you from succeeding. Do not be afraid of failing. When you first learned to read it took a while to get those A B C's but now you can master this simple book from those earlier attempts. Where your heart is, so is your success.

PRINCIPLE SIX:
DREAMS / GOALS

*A dream is something you think you can do,
a goal is something you are doing.*

Those with status will never change the status quo, The culture of success or the culture of failure, will protect itself. We should turn more of our dreams into goals and then our goals into plans. A dream is something you think would be nice to do. A goal is something you think you can do.

A plan is something you are doing. Successful people seldom seek change. Your business is like your child. You raise it to take care of you in your old age. You would not allow a child molester to baby sit your children just because he or she knew great bedtime stories. So why allow folks into your business and professional life just because you knew them in high school or because they are your cousin? The child needs development and attention and it has to come from you.

MAINTAINING AND GAINING

It is important to understand that some people are "Maintaining" and others are "Gaining." There are no rights or wrongs with this; they are two distinctly different priorities in life. You need to understand which category you are in and understand why you may need to change.

Some folks are trying to maintain their position in life, whether it's at their job, income level, or statues in the community. Some people just want to not rock the boat, remain comfortable, and see no problem with where they are in life. They just want things to stay the way they are in their lives and see no reason to change anything.

Those seeking to gain more out of life are not satisfied with where they are in life and are seeking to make changes. They are seeking a better income, a higher education, a different job, or to move out of the old neighborhood. They do not like where they are in life and have no intentions of staying where they are in life.

There are both honorable and common beliefs system, but you cannot live in both at the same time. You will disappoint one group or the other.

You will lose acquaintances, friends, relatives, and even siblings. You can deny it, close your mind to it, and even pretend you can do both. But do not lie to yourself; either you will choose or others will choose.

MAINTAINING You are maintaining where you are, not looking to go forward. You want to stay in the same crowd, doing the same things and going to the same places. But this crowd is not going to support any new ideas or changes.

GAINING You are concentrating on going towards a goal. This will change who you hang out with, not where you hang out. You don't have to change the environment; you may still be in the environment. But you are not hanging out with the party crowd. Now you are hanging out with researchers, engineers, whatever your "business" will be.

"WE ARE COOL BUT WE ARE GOING TO HAVE TO COOL IT!"

You are still my cousin, teammate, friend, and classmate, but I need to get over here and hang with the other business-minded people while you hang with our old friends. You don't even know the people you will go to the top with. They are looking for you as you are looking for them. If you can see it for yourself you can get it for yourself.

Painting of Driveway

Photo of Driveway

This is a Painting and a Photo of my driveway. Look carefully at both. It is a unique driveway, custom built for the home. It is about 85 yards long and curves to the right.

The Painting was done in 1984. That is why the trees are not as full in the Painting as they are in the Photo. The driveway wasn't built until 2007 and I did not buy the home until 2011.

The home is in Missouri, the Painting was in California. This was my vision of my home painted

1,800 miles away and 27 years apart. I had it on my wall, told my wife this was our retirement home and laid out our plans to be prepared for it when God presented it.

My wife and I have a friend who is one of the most beautiful women in California. She was a past San Diego Charger cheerleader and was competing in the Mrs. California beauty pageant. After winning the contest, she proceeded to the national finals for Mrs. America.

Well my friend lost that contest and was very disappointed. My wife and I tried to comfort her because she was beginning to take her rejection personally. At that level of competition every woman was beautiful, talented and sophisticated, but not everyone was what the judges were looking for.

It was like going out on an audition for a play. You may be the most beautiful Japanese actress in the audition, but if they are looking for a blond, blue- eyed European actress, you may not get the job. You can have the most talented trained rabbit in the world, but if the script called for a trained squirrel, you will be disappointed. In a beauty contest, no one knows what the judges are looking for because it all depends upon their individual personality. She lost because she was not exactly what they were looking for. They chose a woman as totally different from her as possible; she was not going to win that contest.

It was not personal; the judges are always different and are looking for different things. You are never rejected personally; the client is looking for something different or you have failed to show him what he needs.

I know many sales training manuals project the thought that people buy from you, if they perceive your belief in the product. That may be true and many of you will try to sell yourself as well as the product. But let's face it; they are not really going to buy you; they are going to buy the service or product.

Many of us learn of a great plan for financial independence and take it on with enthusiasm. We rush out to tell our friends and relatives about it and share the great success you anticipate. Then you look in astonishment as our friends and relatives get more and more confused with your presentation.

They look at you and worry about your mental state or your gullibility in this "crazy" idea. Why? Why is it so easy for you to see the great idea when your close associates cannot?

Maybe it is because you see how it will benefit you, not how it will benefit them. Yes, if I join this multi-level group under you and buy so much product, you may realize your dream of having that boat. Yes, I can see how much you could use my help. The only problem is that I am tired of being used. Do not ever make a presentation to someone without making it clear what the benefit is to them.

PRINCIPLE SEVEN:
TRUTH

Truth is eternal and unchangeable and does not submit itself to the thoughts, hopes, or actions of man.

Stop Whining and Get To Work!

You can only have "self-pride" in your deeds, not those of others. It matters little how great your uncle was or the achievement of your big brother. What are you doing? In the long run we spend too much time making excuses, because of the failure of others. We blame our position in life on our parent's divorce, poverty, bad schools, or some other external force beyond our control. That is the response of a child.

The child depends upon the parent for all needs and wants. Everything the child needs depends upon some action of the parent. If the child is hungry, the parent must act. The child cannot go to bed, dress or go somewhere without total input from the parent. If you are looking to someone else to blame because of the position you have in life, you are still a child and you need to grow up.

It matters little about yesterday; you are in charge of tomorrow. We spend so much time whining about our handicaps that we cannot focus on tomorrow. If you spend all of your time looking back into the past, you may stumble into the future.

Look at the total failure of Abraham Lincoln. By any account he was a complete failure. However, he is considered a hero by many because of his achievements in the midst of his failures.

- He failed as a businessman, as a storekeeper.
- He failed as a farmer; he despised this work.
- He failed in his first attempt to obtain political office.
- When elected to the Legislature he failed when he sought the office of Speaker.
- He failed in his first attempt to run for Congress.
- He failed when he sought the appointment to the United States Land Office.
- He failed when he ran for the United States Senate.
- He failed when friends sought for him the

nomination for the vice-presidency in 1856.

The key to Lincoln's success was how well he handled failure, just as yours will be.

By all accounts Lincoln was a failure!

If you are the fourth generation living in or near poverty, YOU ARE DOING SOMETHING WRONG! Pay attention! it is not "the system;" it is the decisions — decisions your mother made, your grandfather made, and even your great-grandfather. It's decisions resulting in some behavior, and decision-making skills which became your "culture." If this is true, you must face "the truth, right between their lies!"

You must admit to having a "poverty based culture." While you are not responsible for the truth, you are responsible for what you do with the truth. Truth is your friend — a harsh friend at times, but a friend in deed. If "Truth will set you free," then freedom fighters must always seek the truth.

Change your behavior and you will change your culture. Change can be positive or negative, but the truth remains, change your behavior and you will change your culture. Does your honest analysis of your family culture show one based upon poverty or near poverty? Then change your behavior and your learned responses to life. Since all of us are effected in various ways by our history and the history of the community around us, if you change, it will change.

If you live in a region that serves an industry of low wages, you are destined to work in that industry for those wages. If you stay there and hang out with the sons and daughters of the community, getting a job in the industry becomes one of the goals in your life. You have just made a series of decisions that will lead to living in the area you dislike. It will lead to doing the things you dislike doing, with people with whom you have little shared values. The truth will allow choices — good or bad, negative or positive. If you live on a farm and stay in the area, you will be more likely to become a farmer or work in that industry. If you do not want to live in that culture, you must leave the farm; it will not leave you.

Rejection causes no pain; only our self-induced mental punishment causes pain. We think someone has rejected us when they reject our great idea, product or service. They have not rejected us; they have rejected themselves or our poor presentation of what we represent. The idea is to remember what is being presented and what is being rejected. Only the topic can be presented and only the topic can be rejected.

The truth is absolute. It is not relative, does not depend upon your confidence, and cannot be persuaded by effort. It is also not effected by your level of confidence. The truth is not as you see it; the truth is as it is. If you do not know the truth when you find it, you will follow the one with the greatest lie.

Truth is as it is. The Nazi Army were confident that they would conquer and rule the world. The Japanese Imperial Navy were confident that they would defeat the American Fleet. The truth is they did not. Study for the truth with an honest heart. The truth will set you free, but only if you are not afraid of what you will discover.

The truth can be painful, scary, disappointing or embarrassing, but it is never weak, nonproductive, or negative. Seek it, make it your friend. Search for it and never doubt where it will lead you. Truth is eternal and unchangeable and does not submit itself to the thoughts, hopes, or actions of man.

Looking back on all of the advice I received from folks who did not know me, I have discovered the TRUTH! It wasn't true that I was a slow learner, stutterer or poor child. It was not true that I was disabled, unable to work or take care of myself. It was not true that I could never own a home, business, or become an author. I discovered what the real truth was. The real truth was what I called myself, not what others called me.

The truth will reveal things to you and about you. The truth revealed to me that success comes from being consistent, persistent, and never giving up. The truth revealed to me the importance of never ceasing to learn, never ceasing to associate with like-minded people, and never ceasing to give to others.

The truth revealed to me two distinct cultures: the culture of success and the culture of failure. They cannot be blended; they cannot be given equal time and you cannot make them work together. You get the one you feed the most. The truth revealed to me that I needed to have supreme confidence in my success, even though others had supreme confidence in my failure.

There seems to be a notion of "fairness" that is assumed in many aspects of our lives. "That's not balanced," seems to be the mantra. Do we really want to be "balanced," or do we want truthfulness? With modern man finding it more and more difficult to distinguish right from wrong, we can only seek balance in ideas — those right and those wrong. However, if there is truly good and evil, right from wrong, or truth and lies, then we must seek them out and honor what is honorable and reject that which is dishonorable.

If not, we will find ourselves seeking more lies, to balance what we know is the truth. We will be judging a situation for our own good and determine that we need more lies to balance the truth. Or we will conclude that more evil must be brought in to balance the good we have found. We are foolishly looking for a balance between evil and good. That is very strange.

This new "tolerance" in our culture has turned into "acceptance" of very alternative points of view. We now hold different views to the same level as our own views and consider that to be the optimum human expression of civility. However, if I hold your principles to the same level as mine, then I would have no principles at all. If I believe that we should not give condoms to children and you believe we should, how can I hold your belief as equal to mine? I would have to compromise on my own principles, to make you comfortable with yours. You and I may be able to work, live and socialize together, but never on this issue.

CONCLUSIONS

I needed friends and associates who supported my belief in self-determination. It was necessary to have a support system in place to keep me motivated and give me knowledge. How can you work on your own business if all of your friends and associates believe owning a business is impossible? They would take every opportunity to discourage you, never encourage you. They would only participate in your business by occasionally borrowing money from you. These old friends would not even buy from you. They do not mean you any harm, but success is not of their culture, managing failure is. They cannot understand your willingness to sacrifice your "spare time" to pursue your own business. They cannot understand why you are no longer hanging out and waiting for Monday morning to pick more cotton. They may never understand and it is not personal.

There are times when we must leave old friends behind. I will see them at reunions, funerals and weddings. But my time is spent with those of the same dream. If I changed political parties or religious faith, it would result in a change of association. It does not mean you treat your old friends differently. It simply means you do not have the same beliefs or standards as they do. If you joined gamblers or alcoholics anonymous you probably would not still hang out with your friends at the casino or the bar. You would meet new friends who support your beliefs. It is the same with economics. If you want to change where you are going, change what you are doing and with whom you are doing it.

You must change your actions from defensive to offensive. If you think "they" are out to get you and "they" will keep you down, then "they" have more power over your life than you do. If you perceive others as having more influence over your life than you do, you will develop a defensive life style. Your main source of power is your ability to protest, and demand from the stronger groups, benefits for the weaker groups. Otherwise, your life will be full of self-doubts and inaction. You will always be concerned about who has done you wrong. Others will look at you the same way you look at yourself. If you think you're inferior, you will be treated that way. When I walk into a business I do not wonder if they like black people or respect me as a person. I act like I own the place and in most places, they treat me that way.

Once the anger was gone, all I had left was confidence. It stopped being the fault of others and it became my responsibility. My actions became more positive in response to my self- perceptions. If I needed something, I must be the one to act, no one else.

This concept changed my language. I began to speak in certain positive terms. I did not call them positive terms, but looking back now I recognized that is what they were. I stopped saying things in negative terms. "If they would leave me alone, I could make it" became "I will make it." NO excuses; no blame. "Why can't I?" became "When will I?" "They (the enemy, the man or the system)" became secondary to things I had control over. Reading good books, listening to good tapes and being around good people were in my control.

There is something else about success. It tends to be cultural. There is a culture of poverty and a culture of prosperity. If you identify it as a culture it's easier to recognize. However, if we identify this as a racial, economical, or religious culture, others who do not belong to the same groupings will find it harder to embrace the culture of success.

For example, in America, part of the culture of success is speaking the English language properly. It may not be righteous, tolerant nor justified but there is a cultural language for success. Mastering the English language is important if you wish to work in corporate America or anywhere else in this country.

The Rap industry makes millions of dollars for its artist and producers. Most of the language is not standard English but slang. Within the industry you can achieve some high level of success and still not master the English language. However, the Rap stars speak perfect English when it comes time to sign record deals or negotiate with a tennis shoe company. They may speak in "Rap-ese" at the award ceremonies but catch them talking to their lawyer. It becomes a frank, plain discourse in the strictest English language.

All cultural groups protects their own system. Everything from organized crime to The Boy Scouts has its own rules and attitudes and they are all protected by their systems. If you are going to be a leader, you may have to change the system, develop your own system, or conform to the system you are in. You could be the world's best Country Western Blues Singer but it would be very hard to break into the business. Can you imagine the obstacles you would face traveling to Nashville, Tennessee trying to break into Country Music as a Blues singer?

It is not impossible, but you would experience rejection and criticism, because the culture that has nurtured the Country Music business will protect itself from change. Even "Rap" had to establish its own identity before it became mainstream. Someone had to change the culture, or make a new one. Your success in life may require you to do the same thing. Surround yourself with "like-minded" people. Not just people you like, not people who mind you. You need like-minded people to guide and support your goals. Knowledge is power and you get knowledge from experience. The best knowledge is gained from the experiences of others because they have also made the mistakes.

With "self-confidence" it no longer mattered if someone did not like me or want me to succeed. It only mattered that I intended to succeed. We are often defeated by defeat.

If one had been told that defeat is his destiny and victory is hopeless, he may still act. There may be some timid attempt to try anyway, even with the voice of defeat ringing in the ears. Even with the courage to try, in the face of everyone's expectation, one can be discouraged by a simple defeat. We tend to try only once and give up after the first defeat. We retreat back to the comfort of those who tried to discourage us from trying.

The four-minute mile was not broken the very first time tried. Scientists, doctors, trainers and other athletes continued to express the hopelessness of trying to break the four-minute mile record.

After constant defeat, it was broken and has now been shattered. During the horse-and-buggy days, it was thought that the human body could not stand the physical pressure of traveling over 55 miles per hour. Breaking the sound barrier, crossing the Atlantic in a hot air balloon, and swimming across the English Channel were accomplished after many defeats. Defeat builds character and gives answer to what not to do.

A little baby learns to walk when it gets tired of crawling. The child will not be successful in learning to walk the first time it tries. It will continue to fall down, continue to fail, until it gets tired of falling down. The child does not walk after mother teaches walking skills.

After conquering defeat, the child then tries running and falls down. Often, the child falls many times, yet continues to try. The child will not learn to run until it gets tired of skinning its knees in failure. If the parent keeps the child safely in their arms and prevents it from failing, the child will enter adolescence not knowing how to walk. Success in walking and most other things comes from working through failure.

The most successful sales personnel will be the ones with the most failures. By simple numbers, they have been in the game more often and, thus, have realized more success. Some of us count failures other count success. Babe Ruth was not only the most successful home run hitter of his era, he was also the strike-out king. Either way you look at him, failure or success all came from getting into the game. Many of you are so afraid of the game that you never play. Success comes in "can" and "cannot." The failure does not make you a failure unless it stops you from continuing. Someone once said that it was the staying down not the falling down which defeats us.

At 21, I was unemployable, disabled, but not discouraged. I laid in a hospital bed, unable to feed myself or speak above a whisper, and I knew I had just two choices: give up and accept the disability everyone was talking about, or get my behind out of that bed and find some other way to earn a living.

Success is in the trying and the continuation of trying. My goal was simple: go to law school and graduate. I had to fight through the rehabilitation, the pain, and then school. I had to fight for a job and I continue to fight today. I passed the Law School Admission Test (LSAT) four years after laying in that hospital bed. I decided not to go on to law school, but the successes in my life can be traced back to that goal.

When I walked out of the LSAT that December of 1974, I looked back on August 11, 1971. I was about to graduate from UC Berkeley, I had defeated the physical obstacles facing me, and I had changed my destiny, with determination. But most of the success came from failure.

I could fill this book with the failed attempts to graduate from one of the toughest schools in the nation. Most times, my physical discomfort won the morning "should I get up" game. The medication interfered with my social and academic life, and I was always making up classes and assignments, because of my physical limitations.

But nothing was going to stop me. I did not ever seriously consider quitting nor redirecting myself. Every obstacle and every defeat was simply a lesson learned. It was analyzed and put away for future use.

When I looked back I noticed something. It occurred to me that everyone calling for my defeat was simply afraid of their own success. I was the first in my family to go into the military, college, or business. Many people assumed that since it had never been done we could not do it. My physical condition gave me no choice. Even if it had never been done, I had to do it. There were no other choices: failure or success, give up or keep trying. My choices were pretty contrasting. Walk or lay in bed forever. Struggle or sink. Allow the failure to rule you or you rule the failures. I had no choices; neither do you.

You cannot succeed by destiny; you must succeed by determination. Destiny would be too easy. Success by destiny could be achieved without effort, sacrifice or determination. All of these seem to predetermine the level of success. Most highly successful people became successful when it seemed their destiny called for failure.

If you lay in bed long enough you are destined to get bed sores. If you say you cannot do something long enough you are destined to fail. I control my destiny; it does not control me. So many people who were born with declared birth defects overcame them to achieve athletic, social, and business success.

President Roosevelt was paralyzed with polio and Helen Keller could not see nor hear, yet both reached the very height of success. President Roosevelt was not destined to be president but he certainly was determined to be.

If you want success and freedom, look at the habits and traditions you keep. If you want a change in your life-style, you must change your life. It does not matter what kind of change you want. Weather you "turn it over to Jesus" or "become one with nature," it will require some changes in life before you get a change of life-styles.

This is why this message is so important to new business owners. If you are new to business, most of your current associates are probably not business owners. Most likely, they are doing the same things you have been doing; that is why you are their friends. You have decided to make a change and you've begun your own business. As your business grows you will find yourself spending more time with other business owners. You have changed your behavior and it has changed your culture. You may not have changed income levels, because of the cost of running a new business, but how you spend, invest, and think about money have changed.

Think it or believe it? If you just "think you can, one day" and do nothing else, it was only a thought. If you believe you can and need to, you will make plans today that will bring your belief to you. No belief, no action; no action, no success.

Probabilities or possibilities. Many people go through life making decisions (or in most cases, non-decisions) based upon the possibilities available. Think about it; almost everything is possible and you will follow the positive possibilities only.

It is possible to win the lottery, so you play every weekend because "you never know."

Well, it is also possible to lose every weekend and it never seems to stop you from playing. However, because the "PROBABILITIES" of winning the lottery is very low, most of us will not spend every paycheck on tickets. It is the probabilities, not the possibilities that keep us in check.

We would rather rely upon "luck," as if something about our strong personalities or the relationship we have with our inner consciousness can have a profound effect on matter? However, a reality check will demonstrate that most success around us was achieved by people who did certain things a certain way for a certain period of time. The possibilities of us achieving similar success is increased by following the same patterns of these leaders. But our human ego gets in the way, and many of us would rather spend years trying it "our way."

Instead of building your business with people who have shown their probabilities, we hang on to every dedicated incompetent associate because of the possibility that they may change. If you have to wait until someone grows into their position, you will have to wait before you can make a decision. What do you want in your business, employees who are learning the business or those who are doing business? Make decisions and get busy.

"Haste makes waste" does not mean stop moving. It means slow down and make rational decisions based upon probabilities, not just possibilities. It means making a good analysis based on past evidence, then aggressively going ahead.

Stop thinking about it and start doing it.

Fear of failure brings about fear of starting, and that is failure. Failure is not your enemy, procrastination is. We spend a great deal of time getting ready to get ready and never get started. You have read the book and feel inspired, now get busy. Do not just read it and become inspired to change your habits and just think about it. Put down this book and get started. Success is waiting for you. Learn to appreciate the lessons in failure; they lead to the blessings of success. Let's go win!

NOTES: